CONTENTS

TOWN AND CITY

Hell is a city much like London –
A populous and a smoky city.

Peter Bell the Third, Percy Bysshe Shelley, 1819

QUEEN VICTORIA'S REIGN was a long one, lasting from 1837 to 1901, and during this time, due to huge changes in technology at home and the growth of an Empire abroad, the profile of Britain was altered for ever. It went from being an agricultural nation to an industrialised one, and in that process there emerged a wealthy middle class of industrialists and businessmen as well as a poor underclass who had moved from labouring on the land to labouring in the factories. By the end of Victoria's reign, four-fifths of her people lived in towns and the population had doubled in nearly half a century: a third of that population was aged under fifteen.

While the child's lot differed depending on the area in which he or she lived – be it a mill town, port or market town – the places where the worst conditions and the most extreme circumstances applied were in the big cities and, in particular, London. It was in London that the biggest increase in population took place: by 1901, the city contained a fifth of the population of England and Wales. But even in the poor East End of London, there were differences. Charles Booth's survey of 1889 showed that in Mile End the poverty level was 24.6 per cent but rose to 58.7 per cent in Bethnal Green. This demonstrates that life in the East End ranged from working-class households with basic amenities, where the children were clean and healthy, to the destitute living in the workhouse or on the streets, with children often fending for themselves.

The move to the towns and cities had been rapid and the housing built to accommodate the influx was constructed quickly and badly. Most of it was terraced housing, sometimes 'back to back' where the rear and side walls were shared, giving very little light and circulating air. Each house was small and invariably overcrowded, with two families in one house. The outside privy

Opposite:
These homes, only 2.74 metres apart, show the cramped housing conditions of the working class in Bethnal Green. Residents included fish curers and costermongers.

Children played in the streets because there was no room indoors. The boy here is drawing a spiral in chalk on the pavement.

was shared with several other families and water for drinking was drawn from a standpipe. There were few drains and no sewers, and this led to several outbreaks of cholera mid-century. The epitaph of Dr John Snow, a renowned doctor who administered chloroform to Queen Victoria at the birth of her youngest children, reads, '[he] demonstrated that cholera is communicated by contaminated water'. Unfortunately this did not prevent some twelve-thousand people dying of the disease in London during the epidemic of 1853–4. The Government realised the health hazards posed by the slum dwellings and passed the Public Health Act of 1875, which required local authorities to implement building regulations, in which each house should be self-contained, with its own sanitation and water. This change in the design of housing complemented the public investment in sewers and water supply and the result was a general improvement in urban health.

Working-class families were large and the elder children, especially the girls, were expected to look after the younger ones and do household tasks including the washing and cooking. The family diet consisted mainly of bread, potatoes, soup and a little bacon. Food was often adulterated, for instance

A group of children watch as two young boys with makeshift gloves and no shoes box each other in the street.

milk diluted with water, or tea with charcoal. Poor diets and bug infestations were detrimental to youngsters' health, and overcrowding meant that epidemics could spread quickly. It is no wonder that young children did not survive very long; during the Victorian era 40 per cent of annual deaths in England and Wales were children under the age of five.

When mothers went out to work in the mills, for example, an older child, grandmother or neighbour took care of the younger ones. Babies were sometimes given opiates to keep them quiet, which over time could kill them and certainly harm them physically and mentally. When the mother worked at home, the children were usually roped in to help. If she did laundry, for instance, they might do the mangling or deliver the finished articles. But there were trades carried on at home that had a deleterious effect on everyone's health, such as rag-picking, which was dirty, and rabbit-pulling, which filled the air – and lungs – with fluff. A common trade for youngsters

Children play marbles in New Wynd, Hamilton. The end cottage was thatched with bundles of straw and the gas lamps were lit every night and put out in the morning.

Matchbox-making was the lowest paid home work. Women and young children spent twelve hours a day, pasting together strips of paper and wood to form lids and trays, and paying for their own paste and fire to dry the boxes.

at home was matchbox-making. In 1865, Annie Macpherson, who dedicated her life to helping destitute children in the East End, was spurred into action by discovering that children as young as three had given up their childhood to earn three farthings for every twelve-dozen boxes made. 'The infant now makes several hundred boxes every day of her life and her earnings suffice to pay the rent of the miserable room which her family inhabits.' Macpherson publicised their plight and was able to raise money to arrange evening religious classes where a meal was provided.

Life was precarious for the working-class family because its situation could deteriorate easily through ill health or the death of a parent. In 1861, it was estimated that by the age of ten, eleven per cent of children had lost one parent and 1 per cent had lost both. A widow had little recourse to help. She could appeal to various charities providing different goods such as coal in the winter, or clothing, or by attending a mission she and her children might be fed. Children could obtain food by collecting bags of bones from a slaughterhouse or stale bread from the baker; or they might earn pennies by running errands or standing in line at the pawn shop for a neighbour. Most widows, however, turned for help to the Poor Law union ('union' was the name given to groups of parishes that had joined together to provide workhouses). The allowance given by Poor Law authorities was decided by the board of guardians and differed from place to place. Bradford was exceptionally generous in giving five shillings a week to a widow; most unions gave much less. The labour leader, Will Crooks, came from Poplar in the East End where, in 1860, his mother had an allowance of three shillings and some loaves of bread each week because his father had been crippled by a work accident. Unfortunately they were investigated by the guardians who said that Will, at the age of eight, should be earning his own living. They decided to take away the allowance and send the children and father to the workhouse instead. It was cheaper on the rates.

When Charles Dickens wrote *Oliver Twist* in 1837, there were large numbers of children living in the workhouse. Many of them were orphans like Oliver, or children of widows, or had parents in the workhouse. Living conditions in the workhouse were meant to discourage people from going there and for children life was harsh, characterised by loneliness, violence and lack of any emotional support. The children were separated from their parents in the workhouse, although they were allowed to see them on Sundays, for 'an hour of unspeakable joy ... a reminder of home and

Women had very few ways of earning a living and were frequently evicted. This woman has been thrown onto the street with her two small children and her few possessions. She may well have had to go into the workhouse.

humanities outside', as expressed by an inmate, Charles Shaw. The poor food rations meted out to the hungry Oliver reflect the reality of what pauper children could expect at mealtimes, and at night many would cry themselves to sleep under the bed covers.

In 1896, Charles Chaplin, aged seven, with his brother Sydney, was moved from the Lambeth workhouse to the Central London District School in Hanwell, Middlesex. He wrote, 'The first few days I was lost and miserable, for at the workhouse I always felt that mother was nearby, which was comforting.' His mother sometimes visited them. On one occasion he had ringworm and was ashamed of his head, shaved and smothered in iodine, but 'Mother laughed, and how well I remember her endearing words... "With all thy dirt I love thee still".' Unfortunately his mother's mental state deteriorated and after three years the boys were released into the custody of their father, who died two years later. But by that time, the twelve-year-old Chaplin had joined a troupe of tap-dancers.

When the time came to leave the workhouse, the children were found employment by the guardians. Boys went into the army, navy, or were apprenticed as shoemakers, tailors or fishermen. The girls went into domestic service, where they were sometimes badly mistreated: in 1891, a fourteen-year-old ex-workhouse girl was beaten to death by her mistress in South Shields. Girls'

The Central London District School was built in Hanwell in 1857, funded by the City of London, the East End and the St Saviour's unions. Charles Chaplin was its most famous pupil, supposedly seated at the right front table, fourth from the gangway, in the dining hall decorated for the Queen's Diamond Jubilee in 1897.

Friendly Societies were set up to give lodging and support to girls looking for work.

There were some destitute children that even the Poor Law missed, and these were taken in by charitable institutions established by individual philanthropists, such as Annie Macpherson and Dr Barnardo, or by the Church, such as the Anglican Waifs and Strays Society. Barnardo at first limited himself to numbers he could afford to support, but when a boy was found dead from cold and starvation a few days after Barnardo had turned him away, a notice went up outside his Stepney Home saying 'No destitute child is ever refused admittance'. Barnardo's ingenuity in raising funds knew no bounds: he founded brigades of boys to deliver messages or

chop wood; he wrote human interest stories, asking for donations; and he sold 'before and after' photos to show how pauper children had benefited from his care. Nonetheless, there were always too many children who needed his help. His solution was to do what Annie Macpherson had done – send children to Canada. He believed that 'what was needed in order to give them the opportunity they had missed … was, in a very real sense, a new heaven and new earth – the fresh conditions of a colonial life.'

He set up a system of emigration in which children went by boat to receiving homes in western Canada, from where they were placed on farms to help the farmers. Although he tried to ensure that the children were properly looked

The unions would advertise in the local newspaper when workhouse girls were ready for employment in domestic service. When a girl left to take up work as a maid, she was given a set of clothes to take with her.

after, it was difficult to check up on children spread out on isolated farms throughout Ontario and Quebec. As a result many children were treated as overworked servants and lacked affection, although others found families in which they were loved and cared for. In fact, out of the one hundred thousand British children who were sent to Canada, most of them made their lives there: it is their descendants who today make up 11 per cent of the Canadian population.

This boy was rescued from the streets by Barnardo. 'Before and after' pictures were used by Barnardo to show how his homes helped children and thereby raise funds.

COUNTRY LIFE

They worked on hour after hour, unconscious of the forlorn aspect they bore
in the landscape, not thinking of the justice or injustice of their lot ... In the
afternoon the rain came on again, and Marian said they need not work any
more. But if they did not work they would not be paid; so they worked on.

Tess of the D'Urbervilles, Thomas Hardy, 1891

SOCIETY in the country was divided quite simply into rich and poor: the
wealthy landowners and the impoverished labourers, with a few small
farmers in between. The relationship between the landowner and his
labourers was reminiscent of medieval times. At the end of the nineteenth
century Joseph Arch, who founded the National Agricultural Labourers'
Union, wrote: 'There was the squire, with his hand of iron overshadowing us
all. There was no velvet glove on that hard hand, as many a poor man found
to his hurt... He lorded it right feudally over his tenants.'

Throughout the early years of Victoria's reign, life was very hard for the
rural poor because the landlords appropriated common land that the labourers
had used for their own animals. In the Highlands of Scotland and Ireland, farm
workers continued to be cleared off the land to make way for grazing
livestock. Many country people had to move to the towns to find work in the
factories, mills and mines: in 1851, 21.7 per cent of the population worked
in agriculture but by the end of the century this figure had halved.

Labourers' families were so poor that children were put to work as soon
as they were able. Although their pay was very low, together with what their
mother earned it was enough to make a substantial difference to a family
living on the breadline. When Queen Victoria came to the throne, the average
weekly wage for a farm worker was about thirteen shillings, which could be
increased to nearly £1 if the woman and children also worked. (£1 in 1850
was equivalent to about £60 today.)

Living conditions for the majority of families were appalling. The
cottage had to house the parents and their four to six children, plus a

Opposite:
Mrs Wickham and
her family, in 1864,
are seated outside
their cottage. Farm
labourers' cottages
were small, often
one room in which
the family slept
and ate.

The children of wealthy landed families had plenty of leisure time in the summer and enjoyed the new pastime of cycling that became popular in the 1890s.

Cottage industries, such as spinning yarn, brought in necessary income and children were taught skills from an early age.

grandparent, usually in one room. There was hardly any furniture – perhaps a few stools and an iron pot in which to cook, and the roof often leaked. A Mr and Mrs Hall travelling in Ireland in the 1840s described the cottages thus:

Carding wool and Spinning with a Castle wheel

Most of them consist of only one room, in which the whole family eat and sleep; there is generally a truckle bed in the corner for the owner, or the grandparents but the other members of the family commonly rest upon straw or heather, laid on the floor, covered with a blanket, if they have one, and the clothes of the sleepers ...The Pig – the never absent guest – a cow if there be one – and occasionally a few fowl, occupy the same room at night ... The dung-heap is invariably found close to every door – usually right across the entrance, so that a few stepping stones are placed to pass over it.

Feeding and clothing the children was a perpetual problem. The children wore hand-me-down clothes, but the most expensive item was their boots – without these they were not allowed in school. The leather was so hard it rubbed their feet raw and children sometimes had to miss school because of sore feet. Their diet consisted mainly of bread and dripping and weak tea, with a few vegetables from the family plot. A young ploughboy born in 1886 described what he ate: 'I lived on fat pork for twelve months... That's all we had for breakfast, dinner and tea.' Fat pork was the fat from the pork, not the meat. Some children went poaching for fish or rabbits with their father when there was no money for food, although they risked deportation if they were caught.

Children often worked together with their mother and other women and children. They were given the most tedious and backbreaking tasks, such

These boys were lucky enough to be apprenticed to a smithy, where they learned skills such as welding, shoeing and toolmaking.

A nursemaid wheels her young charge round the farmyard. Country girls were mainly employed in domestic work in the homes of affluent farmers.

This young ploughman was only eleven years old when the photograph was taken, but had been working a plough since he was nine.

as clearing the ground of stones and weeds, spreading manure, hoeing turnips, and lifting potatoes, and their work was carried out in all weathers. Depending on the time of year, young boys would help the carter or ploughman, or scare away the birds in the newly sown fields. Scaring birds was a lonely, boring job, lasting from dawn to dusk, which a young child did alone. His ragged clothes gave rise to the appearance of the scarecrow found today in children's illustrations and occasionally in the fields.

The corn and hay harvest time was when the women and children were needed most and the schools emptied, only to be filled again after the harvest was over. More was paid for harvest work than any other, but even so the wages paid to the women were only half that of the men, and children were naturally paid even less. The children helped in a variety of ways: they looked after the younger children, so that their mother could work in the fields till all hours; they carried food and drink out to the harvesters; and they helped to bind the sheaves and stack them. After the crop had been harvested, the women and children went into the fields to gather what had been left behind. This would be threshed and then ground, and the resultant flour kept the family in bread for a couple of months.

Work was harsh for children of a young age, and yet people believed that children, particularly boys, should start to work early: this would make them grow into strong and efficient farmers. In fact the opposite was true. Doing heavy manual labour overworked growing muscles and prevented them from

Hop-picking was very labour intensive and employed children during the season. Families from London's East End would go hop-picking to earn money and enjoy the country air at the same time.

"HOP-PICKING. TALLYING OFF.   38"

These young girls are playing at rabbiting, imitating the gamekeeper whom they have watched catching rabbits on their father's land.

This young farm labourer is posing in a traditional smock with a pitchfork, ready for haymaking.

developing properly; this told on them when they were adults. They were also vulnerable to tuberculosis.

The way in which children were employed differed according to farming conditions in different parts of the country. As far back as 1656, the system of female 'bondagers' was practised in the Borders villages and Northumberland, in which a male labourer was bound to provide a female labourer as part of his condition of service. She was often a child, since the minimum age was about ten, and had to be on call to work in the fields whenever required, in all weathers, as well as during the harvest. Her work was regarded as paying the rent of the family cottage. Fortunately, by the end of the nineteenth century, this system had fallen into disuse.

However, the most notorious of systems was in play during the 1850s and '60s in the eastern counties of England: the system of employing women and children in gangs. The Sixth Report of the Children's Employment Commission stated that 'an analysis of returns from a number of parishes showed that 1,636 children were employed under the age of thirteen, of whom 871 were males and 765 females.' The Commissioner said he had found twenty children employed under the age of seven, but some began work as early as five. 'Boys and girls of this tender age went five or six miles to their work and the same distance back ... Children were sometimes called up at half past five in the morning, and did not return home till seven or eight o'clock at night. Their wages were in Suffolk as low as 2d or 3d a day; and one woman stated that "Frank was six years old when he went out. He got 1½d a day the first year, and was raised 1½d a day each year. Agnes, seven years old, got 2d".' They cleared the fields of stones and weeds and planted potatoes; once they had finished on one farm, they were moved to another.

The gangmasters were described as 'convicted felons and thieves and men who had committed gross and indecent assaults on members of their gangs'. Their earnings were dependent on how much their gang worked so they worked them hard, often kicking and beating the young ones so that they kept up with the others. A tradesman of Chatteris, in his evidence before the Royal Commissioners, said 'the death-rate in that district of children under two years was very great ... out of seventy-two burials in the year, thirty of them were children of one year old and under.' He believed that

Families would often specialise in a particular skill. Here a family is stripping willows to make eel traps.

19

Punch and Judy, a traditional, popular glove puppet entertainment, was a travelling show, which stopped to perform at villages and country towns.

the reason was the drugging of babies with opium to keep them asleep so that the mother could do her work.

Both public opinion and Parliament were outraged. Mr Dent, MP for Scarborough, tabled a motion to regulate the employment of women and children in agriculture and the result was the Gangs Act of 1867. It required that all gangmasters be licensed by a magistrate, prohibited mixed gangs of men and women, and no child under the age of eight was allowed to work in a public agricultural gang. While this went some way to improving conditions, it did not protect young children over the age of eight or children working in other agricultural employment. It was only when the Education Act of 1876 was passed, making schooling both compulsory and full-time for children aged five to ten and part-time till the age of fourteen, that inroads were made into the employment of children in agriculture.

Although life was hard, children were very much part of a family and stayed with one or other of their parents most of the time. They occasionally had time off, to enjoy the local fairs for example. It was reported of Haddenham, Buckinghamshire, that 'no institution was more popular, or deeply rooted in village sentiment than our annual Feast.' The May Day festival was mainly celebrated with children's games and processions, and at Christmas everyone made an effort to ensure there was something special for the table. There were Sunday School outings, or groups going blackberrying – all these provided a welcome rest from work and a chance for children to be themselves.

The Scottish summers were all-too short but children made the most of them. Here a group watch races run in bare feet along a road.

WEALTHY FAMILIES

Always seek the society of those above yourself ... What is good company?
It is composed of persons of birth, rank, fashion and respectability.

Etiquette Book, Arthur Freeling, 1840

THE VICTORIANS were tremendously snobbish. New money based on trade and industry threatened the old order based on land, and the landowners fought a strong but, eventually, losing battle to prevent their class from being infiltrated by wealthy businessmen and industrialists. Novelist Walter Besant remarked in 1887:

> But men in 'trade' ... could not possibly belong to society. That is to say, that
> if they went to live in the country they were not called upon by the county
> families, and in town they were not admitted by the men into their clubs, or
> by ladies into their houses.

Further down the scale, the expansion of business and finance meant that there was a large increase in the number of clerks and other supporting staff, which formed a rapidly expanding lower middle class, whose aspirations were firmly focused on ascending the social ladder. It was deemed of the upmost importance to maintain one's social status or improve it, and this principle was instilled into children from an early age.

Wealthy and middle-class children were obviously not required to work and therefore their lives differed substantially from their poorer peers. Their parents' expectations of them were that the boys follow in their father's footsteps at the very least, but hopefully become important and powerful men within the realm; the girls were required to make good marriages into other wealthy (or even wealthier) families. Their childhood, therefore, was in preparation for this.

Attitudes of the rich towards their children, whether in county families or those who lived in towns and cities, did not differ – expectations were the

Opposite:
Winter has given these children the opportunity to make an enormous snowball in their back garden in Berwick and proudly pose on it for the camera.

same and so was their treatment of their offspring. The fact that the standard of living had improved allowed rich children a childhood, but it was circumscribed by the relationship between parents and child. This was characterised by formality, particularly in connection with the father, and an emphasis on discipline. The innocence of children was their appealing and redeeming quality and led to a certain sentimentality depicted in paintings, if not acted upon in reality.

The reality was that rich children lived separately from their parents in their own world of the nursery, and the wealthier the parents, the less they knew about the daily routines of their offspring: this was the province of the servants. Looking after a baby was a distasteful job best left to a nurse; the parents only wanted to see the baby for a short while when it was fed, happy and dressed up. Mrs Beeton endorsed this view: she called a nursing child 'a baby vampire', and when bottle-feeding became available, Mrs Beeton, in 1860, pronounced breastfeeding 'unseemly'.

Aspirations of moving up in the world are seen in this family portrait where the father stands proudly in his postman's uniform outside his house with his wife and family dressed up for the occasion.

Parents felt that their role was to instil in their children a sense of morality. In *East Lynne* by Mrs Henry Wood, one of the characters propounds this view:

> Let her [the nurse] have the trouble of the children, their noise, their romping ... But I hope I shall never fail to gather my children round me daily ... for higher purposes: to instil into them Christian and moral duties, to strive to teach them how best to fulfil life's obligations. *This* is a mother's task.

Parents thought that material success was the reward for honesty, goodness and hard work, and the way to achieve that was by obedience to the authority of the parents, who would guide their children along the righteous path. While the child owed obedience to both parents, the figure of authority to whom everyone (including the mother) acquiesced was the father.

Father's needs and wishes were what mattered in the family; his home was his source of comfort where he was not to be troubled, hence the nursery where noisy children were kept away. 'All that your papa wants always, is that you are quiet and out of the way', says the governess to her charges in Mrs Gaskell's *Ruth*. How the children felt and what they might

The Victorian extended family was large, as this photo illustrates. Mr Baxter, sixty-four, the head of the family, was a well-to-do farmer and butcher, and is seen here with his wife, mother-in-law, children and grandchildren.

want to do were very much subordinate to their father's wishes. But while the stereotypical Victorian paterfamilias is portrayed as stern and unbending, this was not always the case. Beatrix Potter was fond of her father but found her mother cold and formidable; Florence Nightingale's father taught her several languages, history, philosophy and mathematics, and treated her as a companion. And the Quaker William Lucas said that 'the good example of parents when they can gain their children's affections' was more important than any set of rules. Nonetheless as head of the household the father was the person in control.

If a child did not listen, it was punished. Corporal punishment was used on children as young as three; other forms of punishment included locking a child in its room or in a cupboard, or making it go to bed without any food. However, as the practice of physically punishing a child lessened through the century, emotional blackmail took its place and children were made to feel bad because in some way they had disappointed their parents – and God.

Religion was an important aspect of life in Victorian families, especially for children as it showed them the importance of being good. The whole family went to church every Sunday and daughters in particular were supposed to do good works, such as accompanying their mother on visits to poor families. They also helped out at Sunday school, or supported national

Victorians used a pony and trap as a means of travelling locally for shopping or visiting friends.

The concept of teenage fashion was completely alien to the Victorians – boys and girls dressed just like their father and mother.

27

Clothes were an important indication of class. Kilts and sailor suits were very fashionable for middle-class boys at the end of the nineteenth century.

This dress is fawn velvet trimmed with silk bows, with a separate overskirt. It dates from about 1870 and was made for a young girl of about five years of age.

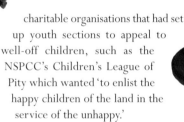

charitable organisations that had set up youth sections to appeal to well-off children, such as the NSPCC's Children's League of Pity which wanted 'to enlist the happy children of the land in the service of the unhappy.'

Religion and morality were what children first learned about at their mother's knee, for that was where most middle-class children began their education; in wealthy homes it was more likely to be nurse's knee. Expectations of what a young child could learn often exceeded a child's capabilities. By the age of seven, boys were sent off to boarding school while girls stayed at home, taught by a governess. If they were not part of a big family they could be lonely, as Beatrix Potter was when her brother Bertram went to school. Governesses were required to teach unrelated chunks of information and to intelligent young girls there seemed no point to many of them, as well illustrated by Elizabeth Barrett Browning's *Aurora Leigh*:

I learnt the royal genealogies
Of Oviedo, the internal laws
Of the Burmese empire, – by how many feet
Mount Chimborazo outsoars Teneriffe…
… because she liked
A general insight into useful facts.

Girls remained in the family home until they were married and the wealthier the family, the more sheltered their lives. Boys went outside the family at an early age when they left for school – and then again when they started work or went to university. Girls had no such rites of passage. They had very little freedom: they couldn't go out without a chaperone and what they were allowed to do was controlled by the family. Since their role in life was to make a good marriage, they were only required to learn insofar as it would help them listen to and understand a man's conversation. 'Her great function is Praise', remarked John Ruskin.

Clever girls must have been very frustrated by attitudes towards them. Their intelligence and knowledge were not valued and any desire to study in depth was considered unnecessary and even injurious to health! Skills such as playing the piano were not for the pleasure of it but because it was useful

Girls were protected from the outside world and spent much of their time at home. They rarely went out without a chaperone.

At a time when the telephone had not yet been invented, social visits ensured that girls kept in touch with their friends and relatives.

The North London Collegiate School for Ladies was the first school to offer girls the same educational opportunities as boys. It also pioneered physical education for girls.

in social situations. They had to defer to the men in their life, including their brothers. A girl's own aspirations beyond marriage were not considered important and she was not taken seriously. The upper class preferred its girls silly and superficial.

There was the option of sending a daughter to a private establishment, a kind of finishing school where she would learn French, music and drawing to give her a little sophistication that might appeal to a future husband. A mid-Victorian critic of girls' education worked out that 640 hours of a girl's time in school was dedicated to arithmetic and 5,520 hours to music. Yet reform was on the way: Frances Buss and Dorothea Beale, pioneers of women's education, helped to prepare girls for more intellectual pursuits. At the age of twenty-three, Frances Buss (1827–94) founded the North London Collegiate School for Ladies and was Headmistress – the first person to call herself so – from 1850 until she died. Dorothea Beale (1831–1906), Head of Cheltenham Ladies' College, founded the first training college for women teachers in 1885. That same year saw Roedean School for Girls opened by three sisters: Dorothy, Penelope and Millicent Lawrence. In the mid-1860s girls were allowed to sit Cambridge Local Examinations for the first time; during the same period, the Schools Inquiry Commission encouraged endowments for girls' grammar schools, which helped them slowly to increase in number. However, these more enlightened schools were rigidly disciplined. Among the school rules at

Good public schools produced the leaders of the country, both civil and military. These officers have been trained at Harrow School.

Cheltenham Ladies' College in the 1880s was the following: 'Leave must be asked from the class teacher before speaking to another pupil. Conversations must be finished in the place where permission is given and may not be carried on in dressing rooms, corridors or staircases.' These rules hardly encouraged an exchange of ideas, intellectual or otherwise.

Parents had a much wider choice of where to send their sons. The great public schools such as Eton and Harrow taught Classics and were attended by the aristocracy, clergy and the top brass of the armed services. The more modern public schools like Marlborough introduced subjects such as science, mathematics and languages to appeal to the professional classes, but the ethos was the same: loyalty, self-discipline, public-spiritedness and a sense of fair play, the latter engendered by the playing of team games such as cricket and rugby. An upwardly mobile industrialist would aim to send his sons to boarding school to escape the connections with their home town and so that they could move in socially superior circles. Professional people from medicine and the law also sent their sons to grammar schools and private schools that taught more modern subjects; Dr Heldenmaier's boarding school in Worksop boasted a chemistry lab, which was very rare in the mid-nineteenth century. Others sent their sons to religious schools – Quakers, for instance, would attend Quaker schools. There were also schools for boys who would leave at the age of fourteen, probably to become clerks, and their education was restricted to figures and how to write a good letter. This was a very limited syllabus, and remained unsatisfactory until a system of secondary education was established under the Education Act of 1902.

Suburbs proliferated around cities to accommodate the growing middle classes. The new rich required a large house for family and servants, and a garden.

CHILDREN AT WORK

In the little world in which children have their existence, whosoever brings them up, there is nothing so finely perceived and so finely felt, as injustice.

Great Expectations, Charles Dickens, 1860

THE VICTORIAN ERA is well known for its exploitation of child labour. Children in the country had always worked alongside the parents in the fields, but when the families moved to the towns and took employment in factories, the children continued to work to help supplement the family income. Even Prince Albert regarded the child of a working-class family as part of its productive power and that the lack of the child's income would 'almost paralyse [their] domestic existence'. Although reformers awakened the conscience of society and dubbed child exploitation immoral, nevertheless during most of the nineteenth century, it was considered good that working-class children went out to work regularly as this helped to prepare them for the adult world.

The textile industry in the north of England was the first to become mechanised in the late eighteenth century. Before the 1770s, textile manufacture was a cottage industry and children helped their parents in the home. The mother spun the yarn, the children would card and wind it and, finally, the father wove the yarn into cloth. Although the children worked with their parents, they had time to go out and play and remained in their home environment.

By the beginning of the nineteenth century, children were in full-time work in the mills, many of them as young as seven years old. For centuries children had worked alongside their parents in the domestic industry, but now they were confined within the mills and worked to the quick rhythm of water- or steam-driven machinery. Some of them were orphans who were given food and shelter in return for their labour. This suited the Poor Law guardians, since the orphans would not have to be supported out of the rates. The child workers

Opposite:
Young cotton mill-workers were called 'half-timers', as by law they had to go to school and therefore only worked in the mill half the day.

'The little match-seller, with ragged clothes and with his bare little feet pattering along at our sides, begs us in piteous tones to buy "a box o' matches, Sir: two hundred and fifty wax-uns for a penny!"' *Walks in and Around London*, 1895.

A young apprentice stands proudly in front of the carcasses on display outside this Victorian butcher's shop.

laboured from Monday to Saturday, 6 a.m. to 7 p.m. with a break for lunch. If they arrived late they were fined and if they fell asleep at work, they were beaten. The factory was very noisy, the dust and fibres in the air damaged their lungs and the bad light their eyes. The foreman watched everyone and if he felt that someone wasn't working hard enough that person would be punished.

Children worked in the textile industry not only because they were cheaper to employ, but also because they were smaller and more agile than adults. Their nimble fingers mended broken threads as they leaned over the spinning machines or they were made to creep under the machines and pick up the loose cotton. Both were dangerous jobs because the heavy, fast-moving machines were not stopped – since this would cost money – so many children were badly injured and some were killed.

When adult factory workers demanded a 10-hour day, their arguments brought to light the hardships of the youngsters working in the mills. Reformers pointed out that those fighting against slavery in the West Indies had a worse case of slavery at home in the form of young textile workers. They also argued that the work would damage children and therefore deplete the adult

Girl cotton mill workers in Manchester enjoying a joke. Female weavers were among the highest-paid female industrial workers.

workforce of the future. In 1833 legislation ended slavery in the West Indies – and in that same year an important Factory Act limiting child employment in the textile industry (except in the silk factories) was passed.

The 1833 Factory Act made it illegal to employ children under nine, and those aged thirteen to eighteen were allowed to work a maximum of 12 hours per day. Children aged nine to thirteen could work for only 9 hours a day and had to attend school for 2 hours a day and present a certificate of attendance before they could work. Thus began the half-time system where the combination of working and schooling, albeit in different proportions, was to continue until the Fisher Act of 1918 ended child employment altogether.

When Victoria ascended the throne in 1837, large numbers of children were employed in the textile industry. Although registration of births came into existence that same year, it only became compulsory in the 1870s, so it was difficult to prove how old a child was. The Factory Act of 1844 limited the hours of work to children aged eight to thirteen to 6½ hours a day and certificates of age were to be granted only by surgeons appointed for the purpose. The number of children and the unsafe conditions in which they (and the adults) worked is brought home by the description in a contemporary news-sheet of the fire in Duncan Street Mill, Rochdale on 3 January 1854:

Henry Radcliffe, one of the mule-spinners, says – I am injured in my back… I do not know whether the rope broke or it was burned by the fire, but I fell upon the floor. I was the last that left the roof of the building, which is four stories [sic] high. There were not less than 13 children came running to me. The flames burst out of the windows, I fastened a rope to a carriage arm. One little girl could not wait while I got the rope ready; she flung herself from the roof of the building. I was sorry for her. We could not get out of the room – the fire and smoke was too great. The children clung to me in despair

Thrusters pushed the tubs of coal from behind with their hands and the tops of their heads. The trapper opened and closed the trapdoors to allow the tubs through and fresh air in.

as if I had been their father. At first I thought we could get down the stairs, but all was in flames. I sent the children off the roof with their pinafores between their hands and the rope. When they had gone I went myself. I got all off except the little one that threw itself off the top of the building.

The textile towns continued to support half-timing – the parents who had worked from a young age themselves saw little value in education and the children liked the independence of earning their own money. But textiles remained an unhealthy industry in which to work – however, that was true of many of the industries in which children worked, particularly mining.

In 1840 a Royal Commission was set up to investigate the working conditions of children in coal mines. They found that children of four, five, and seven years were employed in mining; the youngest sat in the dark for 12 hours a day, opening and shutting doors to allow the large tubs of coal to pass through. The transport of coal required strength and so was performed by older children and women, as described by Friedrich Engels in *The Condition of the Working Class* in England in 1844:

> [They] crawl upon their hands and knees, fastened to the tub by a harness and chain (which frequently passes between the legs), while a man behind pushes with hands and head. The pushing with the head engenders local irritations,

Hurriers wore a harness to pull tubs full of coal, weighing about 600kg, along roadways 60–120cm high from the coal-face to the pit-bottom.

painful swellings, and ulcers. In many cases, too, the shafts are wet, so that these workers have to crawl through dirty or salt water several inches deep, being thus exposed to a special irritation of the skin.

The working conditions were extremely hazardous: fires occurred in one mine or another every day. Dust and gas caused diseases of the lungs which eventually killed miners, and children suffered from stunted growth and deformities, which for women made child-bearing difficult or fatal.

The report was issued in May 1842, and a month later Lord Shaftesbury delivered a speech to Parliament to bring in a Bill to regulate the employment of women and children in mines. In his speech he quoted miner Robert North:

> I went into the pit at seven years of age. When I drew by the girdle and chain, the skin was broken and the blood ran down... If we said anything, they would beat us. I have sometimes pulled till my hips have hurt me so that I have not known what to do with myself.

The Mines Act was passed in 1842 limiting the age of employment of boys to ten years, and banning altogether the employment of women and girls down the mines.

After the 1842 Mines Act, girls were not allowed to be employed underground in mines, but some of them continued to work above ground in a variety of jobs such as sorting coal.

The Children's Employment Commission produced a second report, also dated 1842. This time it looked into dozens of trades, such as bonnet-making, brick-making, calico-printing, chain-making, file-cutting, foundries, glassworks, ironworks, lace-making, lock-making, paper-making, pin-making, potteries, rope-making, and shoe-making. Evidence was collected from personal interviews with hundreds of children and young adults.

William Malum, aged six, was found begging in the streets: 'Works at locks with his father … Does not go to school now; has never a smockfrock, else he should … Never heard of heaven only but once at a Sunday-school.'

Mary Ann Perry, eleven years old, enjoyed working in a pin-making factory for a shilling a week. 'I have only to put pins in paper; it is not a hard job. I come to work at nine o'clock now, go home to dinner at two, have an hour, then work till nine at night … I go to a Sunday school where I learn to spell. I cannot read or write.'

Mary Ann Perry's job was clean, she could sit down and there was a fire in the room. This was comfort indeed! Most children were not so lucky. Charles Shaw, who began working in the potteries aged seven, ran back and

'The shrimps are cried ... from stalls or on rounds, "a penny half-pint, fine fresh s'rimps." ...The females in the shrimp line are the wives, widows, or daughters of costermongers.'
London Labour and the London Poor, 1851.

forth taking full moulds to the 'stove room' to
dry and bringing empty ones to his 'master' –
and woe betide him if he wasn't by his master's
bench at the right moment! He also had to light
the fire in the stove in the morning, crawling
around the works to find available kindling. In
1864 a Factory Act was passed to cover smaller
trades like pottery and percussion-cap making
(with its dangers of explosion), and in 1867 the
Act was extended to the metalworking trades,
such as cutlerymaking in Sheffield, and to
workshops employing fewer than fifty people.
Conditions in workshops were bad as they were
not required to implement the same safety
measures as factories, and inspecting them all
was almost impossible.

The different Acts gave different regulations
for different industries and those children who
fell through the net could always find work in
the brickyards, domestic service or street trading. In the 1850s Henry
Mayhew, a journalist, interviewed people working on the streets of London
including children, such as a nine-year-old girl who sold bootlaces. She had
been selling things for two years already and said she preferred it to staying
at home with nothing to do. Her father was a street musician, her mother

Many newspapers were founded in the Victorian era, for example the *News of the World* (1843) and the *Daily Telegraph* (1855), and there were several editions a day creating plenty of work for newspaper boys.

Children worked in brickyards stacking bricks in kilns or, as here, carrying clay to adult brickmakers. They often covered 8 miles around the brickyard in a day.

worked at shoe-binding and her thirteen-year-old brother in a pottery and although they all worked they could hardly afford a candle and a fire in the winter. Apart from selling, street children could earn a penny in countless other ways:

… tumblers, mud-larks, water-jacks, ballad-singers, bagpipe boys, the variety of street musicians (especially Italian boys with organs), Billingsgate boys or young 'roughs', Covent Garden boys, porters, and shoeblacks … Again: amid the employments of this class maybe mentioned – the going on errands and carrying parcels for persons accidentally met with; holding horses; sweeping crossings (but the best crossings are usually in the possession of adults); carrying trunks for any railway traveller to or from the terminus, and carrying them from an omnibus when the passenger is not put down at his exact destination.

Shoeshine boys earned their living plying their trade on the streets throughout the late nineteenth century. Shoe polish was not commercially available until the early twentieth century.

Many of the one thousand London chimney-sweeps were young boys. Working as a sweep was highly dangerous. Only young children could be used, since only they could fit in the narrow chimney passage. The children were at risk

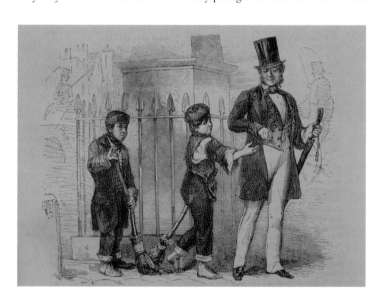

Children could earn a living as crossing sweepers by sweeping London's pedestrian crossings of horse muck and litter to allow the wealthy to cross the street.

from either becoming stuck, or falling and breaking bones or even dying. There was also the health hazard of breathing in soot. Many children were scarred from all the scrapes:

> The flesh must be hardened. This is done by rubbing it chiefly on the elbows and knees with the strongest brine ... close by a hot fire... At first they will come back from their work with their arms and knees streaming with blood... Then they must be rubbed with brine again, and perhaps go off at once to another chimney.

After Charles Kingsley's *The Water Babies* was published in 1863, public opinion demanded action and a year later Parliament imposed a £10 fine for employing child sweeps, which brought the practice to an end.

THE SWEEPS' HOME.
(From a sketch taken on the spot.)

In 1889, the first Act of Parliament for the prevention of cruelty to children, commonly known as the 'Children's Charter' was passed. This enabled British law to intervene, for the first time, in relations between parents and children. Police could arrest anyone found ill-treating a child and obtain a warrant to enter a home if a child was thought to be in danger. The Act also included guidelines on the employment of children, prohibiting boys under fourteen and girls under sixteen from selling goods on the street or licensed premises at night. The state had at long last recognised that children had rights.

Climbing boys were usually parish children. Their task was to clean the inside of the flue with small hand-held brushes and remove the harder tar deposits left by woodsmoke using metal scrapers.

A milkman and his boy would make three rounds a day, selling their milk from open churns.

41

SCHOOLS FOR ALL

More schools are required, and the regular attendance of children
must be secured. Neither of these ... is attainable without compulsion.
In the present state of religious parties, no agreement as to a common
theological instruction can be arrived at, therefore the schools must be
thoroughly unsectarian. Lastly they must be free.

Joseph Chamberlain, Leader of the National Education League, 1870

A T THE BEGINNING of Victoria's reign, there was a division between rich and
poor in education, as there was in everything else. Boys from wealthy
families were sent to schools that had their origins in medieval times (the
most famous public school, Eton, was founded by Henry VI in 1440), and
grammar schools were originally created to teach Latin grammar. However,
the public schools underwent great change during the Victorian period, due
to Thomas Arnold's reform of Rugby School. This is significant because the
values of the public school moulded the leaders of the period and informed
their attitudes and actions.

Arnold believed that the aim of education was the formation of character
and that learning was subservient to this end: 'What we must look for here is,
first, religious and moral principle; secondly, gentlemanly conduct; thirdly,
intellectual ability.' His ideal was to train boys to become Christian gentlemen
first, scholars second. The education of boys in the small society of school was
successful only if they learned how to play their part in the larger society
outside. He allocated responsibility to the boys by creating the prefect system,
emphasising that power should be exercised for good not evil. He updated the
syllabus by introducing mathematics, modern history and modern languages,
and modernised the teaching of Classics by directing attention to literary, moral
or historical questions, encouraging the boys to examine the evidence and think
for themselves. And he replaced field sports with team games like football
to encourage athleticism and instil a sense of fair play and sportsmanship.
His reforms became the basis for the ethos of all Victorian public schools.

Opposite:
A school
photograph with
a difference – while
these young
schoolboys from
Kintyre are posing
in the time-
honoured way,
they do not have
a school uniform.
This was probably
beyond their
parents' means.

Boys and girls lining up for school in Quarter, a mining village in Scotland. The children came from poor families and many of them were not wearing shoes.

Footers Field by John M. Henry, 1887, shows Harrow boys playing football. Harrow School has its own form of football, which is unique to them and is played only in the spring.

Above left: A young Harrovian, Charles Fox, poses in formal dress.

Above right: This is an exhibition of the clothing worn by girls from the Blue School for Girls, a charitable institution in north London; aprons and wide bonnets helped keep the girls clean.

While the upper and middle classes could afford to have their children educated, most working-class families could not and in fact most relied on their children to bring money into the home. Those schools that did exist for poor children were provided by charities and religious organisations,

Above: The cadet movement began in 1859, when Britain feared invasion by France. This cadet corps at Great Ealing School was one of the first – the photo dates from the early 1860s.

the most important of these being the Church of England's National Society, which by 1860 was responsible for three-quarters of the pupils enrolled in public elementary schools. Of the rest, 10 per cent went to the Nonconformist British and Foreign Schools, 5 per cent to Roman Catholic schools and the remainder to those run by Wesleyans, Quakers and other denominations.

Quite a large number of very young children went to 'dame' schools run by an elderly woman, who would teach the children to read and perhaps

the girls to sew while also carrying out her household duties. These schools were popular despite the fee because the classes were small and were held in a house similar to those in which the children lived. They were also flexible, allowing the parents to take the children out of school when they wished and giving them some control over what was taught. By the end of the nineteenth century, mass state-funded elementary education had caused the demise of the 'dame' school.

By far the most regularly attended schools were Sunday schools. Because children worked on weekdays, they were taught on the Sabbath and this appealed to both the religious philanthropists and the industrialists, which may have contributed to the schools' rapid growth: the total number of Sunday schools in Middlesex was 329 in 1833 and 916 in 1858, with a corresponding increase in attendees from 52,121 to 120,823 in the space of twenty-five years. Children were given a basic grounding in reading, writing and religion. Perhaps the Sunday School Union's greatest achievement was to make children familiar with the printed word, since they distributed Bibles, religious tracts and other books in their millions. It is difficult otherwise to evaluate what they did achieve as those children who could read probably learnt it at day-school. However, the religious message came over loud and clear, and the children enjoyed the social activities that were laid on.

There were some children too poor even to attend Sunday school. Charles Dickens described them as 'too ragged, wretched, filthy and forlorn

Opposite bottom: At the age of thirteen, pupil teachers could stay on to help the teachers. At first they were trained by the Head, but later they had to pass an exam to go to training college and become qualified teachers.

These young girls are enjoying a game, dancing round in a circle, in their school playground.

Conformity, not creativity, was what Victorian youngsters were taught in their drawing lesson.

Samplers were pieces of fabric on which young girls practised their needlework skills, sewing letters of the alphabet and flower motifs, amongst other subjects.

to enter any other place.' Lord Shaftesbury was the prime mover in providing Ragged schools in London, but later other urban centres followed suit. In 1844 the Ragged School Union was formed and ten years later, there were 110 schools in London with 1,600 teachers and 13,000 pupils. William Locke, the Union's secretary, described the children who attended the schools:

Most of them are in a very ignorant, destitute, neglected condition, many are quite homeless; many neglected by their parents; many are orphans, outcasts, street beggars, crossing sweepers and little hawkers of things about the streets. We have children of convicts ... of thieves in custody; children of worthless, drunken parents ...

The list goes on. Ragged schools taught reading, writing and arithmetic and often included classes 'to train pupils in the habits of Industry', where girls learned how to sew and cook, while the boys did woodwork and shoe-making. However, there were other important tasks to perform: the children

Children were taught to play instruments and to sing, and would sometimes perform at local events.

were filthy and had to be washed and sometimes their heads shaved to get rid of lice. They were also given clothes, stamped with the name of the school to prevent them being taken to the pawnshop. But most importantly, the children were provided with a simple meal consisting of soup, occasionally meat, bread and cheese, milk and tea. Apart from lessons, outings were arranged, such as day-trips to the seaside or the country, paid for by the Fresh Air Fund.

Although Ragged schools helped destitute children, it was felt that some children were in danger of becoming criminals because of the circumstances in which they lived. Industrial Schools were set up to help these children by removing them from bad influences, giving them an education and teaching them a trade; children who were juvenile offenders were sent to reformatories. Depending on the circumstances of the child, they either attended the Industrial school daily or were able to live in. In 1857 the Industrial Schools Act was passed giving magistrates the power to sentence vagrant children under fourteen to time in an Industrial school. Later, children under fourteen who were vagrants or beggars, or children under twelve who had committed a crime, were sent to the school. The timetable was strict with the children getting up at around 6 a.m. and going to bed at 7 p.m. They were taught 'the three Rs', were given religious instruction, and the boys learned trades such as farming, tailoring and shoe-making while the girls learned sewing, housework and washing, since they were expected to go into domestic service. The Industrial schools were funded from the public purse.

The education of pauper children who lived in workhouses was the Government's responsibility. The Poor Law Amendment Act of 1844 gave

At school, workhouse boys were given lessons in practical subjects, such as metalwork, to fit them for earning a living when they left.

unions and parishes the power to unite and form a school district to establish a large separate school for the education of all the indoor pauper children within that district. For example, in 1849 the Central London School District (which consisted of the City of London, West London, and East London unions, and St Saviour's parish) took over Aubin's School at Norwood. In 1857 the school was moved to a new building in Hanwell, which Charles Chaplin and his brother attended. Outside London, the workhouse might have its own schoolroom, or in some cases children were sent to the local day-school and the guardians paid the fees.

The three Rs formed the basis of Victorian education, with history, geography, art and music thrown in for good measure, and rote learning the form of instruction. Schools were given grants based on the number of pupils who passed exams at the end of the year. Classes were large, so to ensure everyone passed, children had to learn their subjects by repetition rather than understanding. For instance, science was taught as an 'object' lesson where children were given an 'object' like a snail or picture of an elephant to observe and then talk about. However, it was easier for the teacher to make a list of attributes that the children had to learn by rote. This was repeated in geography where children recited the names of countries. Children were also drilled – doing exercises or marching in unison was supposed to teach obedience.

Above: These history cards were used in a card-game to teach youngsters about English monarchs and the important events during their reigns.

Below left: Young children sometimes learnt their letters at their mother's, or in this case, grandmother's knee.

Below right: At the end of the nineteenth century, it was deemed healthy for girls to participate in a little physical exercise at school. Here girls are strengthening their arms by doing exercises with expanders.

There was little sports equipment in Victorian times so children did exercises using sticks or dumbbells. The important thing was to keep in time and follow the teacher's orders.

Discipline was harsh. School punishment books show that children were caned for answering back, sulkiness, being late and throwing ink pellets, among other things. A child who got something wrong could be forced to wear a dunce's cap and stand on a stool in front of everyone to shame him or her. Treatment of children was strict and there was little praise to encourage their efforts.

By the time this photo was taken in 1895, elementary schooling was compulsory – and free – for children up to the age of ten.

The provision of education in England was improved greatly by the 1870 Education Act (named after its author, Liberal MP William Forster). It was the beginning of a national educational system, requiring the establishment of elementary schools nationwide to supplement what was already there – and these schools were to be non-denominational. The country was divided into school districts and where there was little or no school provision, school boards were elected to set up and maintain primary schools in their area; these were known as 'board' schools. The local board had the right to compel children between five and twelve years to attend school and to charge a weekly fee of not more than nine pence; they could also pay the fees if parents were unable to do so. They appointed officers or 'board men' to enforce attendance. Education was not made compulsory because, in rural areas, farmers wanted children to be released from school for harvest and, in the towns, many factory owners wanted to continue to employ children as cheap labour. However, as industry became more sophisticated, factory owners required better-educated people and this was reflected in a series of Acts: in 1880 education became compulsory up to the age of ten (raised to twelve in 1899), and in 1891 it was made free. The absence of real reform in the secondary sector meant that free education in 1900 was generally only up to primary level. In 1902 the Education Act (Balfour Act) gave county authorities power for the first time to provide secondary education out of local rates with the help of grants from central Government.

Higher-grade schools were in existence for a short time at the turn of the century, run by local school boards to give a broader education to those who had reached the top of primary school.

POPULAR PASTIMES

'What is the use of a book,' thought Alice, 'without pictures or conversations?'

Alice's Adventures in Wonderland, Lewis Carroll, 1865

CHILDREN have always managed to find time to play – even those who worked long hours at the start of Victoria's reign spent precious moments playing together in the streets. But as children's working lives became shorter, and young children didn't work at all, more leisure time became available. And although the long school hours curtailed time for play, summer holidays gave children the opportunity to escape the crowded tenements of the city and walk out to the nearest bit of countryside to paddle in streams, catch pond-life and pick flowers on the way home.

The streets and waste ground were the playgrounds of the urban poor. Here they tested their strength by performing handstands, somersaults and other acrobatic feats. Together they played hopscotch, leap-frog, blind man's buff, hide-and-seek, follow-my-leader, tag and many of the games that children play today. While they could not afford to buy toys, an old piece of twine would make a skipping-rope, a kite could be made from a scrap of paper and a stick, and a game of marbles could be played with stones. Occasionally they had rudimentary toys such as a ball, a spinning-top or a wooden hoop, which a child could keep rolling by hitting it with a stick. A woman from Bolton recalled her childhood in the 1880s:

> Boys congregated in groups, particularly playing football and we – the younger element – had to be on guard for the bobby coming, because, you see, you were liable to be fined for playing football in the street in those days.

Children particularly enjoyed days out. Sunday school outings were for many the only opportunity to go into the country or, after the advent of the railways, to the seaside. A woman from Islington in London recalled, 'In 1896

Opposite:
The girl and her younger brother, still in skirts, pictured here with several of their toys – a games racquet, a barrow and a doll – were the children of a Scottish industrialist.

we went from a London station by steam train to Southend. What an adventure that was! My first sight of the sea!' For four years previously, the Sunday School had taken her and her friends in horse-drawn brakes to Epping Forest, 'where we could walk or run on the grass, play games and run races.' A whole day devoted to having fun was freedom indeed.

Excursions were also arranged by the Band of Hope, a temperance organisation for working-class children founded in Leeds in 1847. Members could be enrolled as young as six and met once a week to listen to lectures on the evils of drink and to participate in activities. The latter were often music-based and competitions were held between different Band of Hope choirs. In 1886 three choirs consisting of 1,500 singers performed at Crystal Palace. The Palace had been built for the Great Exhibition of 1851 and everybody visited it, including youngsters with their families. 'Enormous excursion trains daily poured their thousands into the city ... Large numbers of work-people received holidays for the purpose ...' It opened everyone's eyes to the possibilities of manufacturing and trade and was probably the most popular outing of Victoria's reign.

In 1833 the Boys' Brigade was founded in Glasgow and two years later the movement had spread to England. It was aimed at working-class boys aged twelve to seventeen and copied the Salvation Army in combining military muscle with Christianity. Bands were formed to play at the weekly parade night, and soon they were playing at fairs, concerts and other events. This gave working-class boys a chance to learn an instrument and to gain confidence from performing. The Boys' Brigade also instigated camping holidays, the outdoor life instilling a spirit of teamwork and Christian

This early Victorian spinning-top is an elaborate one made of wood and beautifully hand-painted.

Even on a day out at the seaside exploring rock pools, Victorian children had to be well dressed.

These children in their newly knitted outfits are enjoying a family trip on a Clyde steamer.

brotherhood as well as improving the boys' health. Towards the end of the century, boys' brigades had been formed by Jewish, Catholic and Nonconformist groups.

In the last quarter of the century, clubs for unskilled working boys were set up, often in association with public schools and universities. Eton was the first of the public schools to do this in London's East End: its Mallard Street Club was described as a 'Rough Boys' Club' and in 1883 a gentler equivalent, the Selwyn Street Club, was founded. Toynbee Hall was Britain's first university settlement: it was a place where students from Oxford and Cambridge Universities could work among the poor during their holidays. Clubs for working girls were pioneered by Maude Stanley, who founded the

Marching bands, where boys played brass, woodwind and percussion, were popular in the late nineteenth century. Working-class boys could join a band through school or youth organisations.

This doll with a pretty porcelain face was made in France in the 1870s. Dolls were considered appropriate toys for girls, in preparation for motherhood.

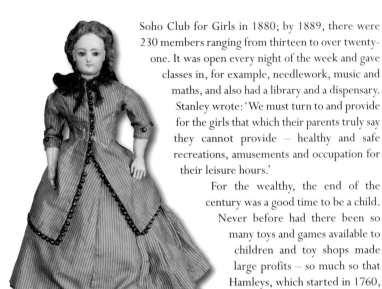

This was a board-game for up to six players who started from the suburbs, such as Hampstead, indicated on the outside of the board, and took fifty moves to reach the Bank of England in the centre.

Soho Club for Girls in 1880; by 1889, there were 230 members ranging from thirteen to over twenty-one. It was open every night of the week and gave classes in, for example, needlework, music and maths, and also had a library and a dispensary. Stanley wrote: 'We must turn to and provide for the girls that which their parents truly say they cannot provide – healthy and safe recreations, amusements and occupation for their leisure hours.'

For the wealthy, the end of the century was a good time to be a child. Never before had there been so many toys and games available to children and toy shops made large profits – so much so that Hamleys, which started in 1760, opened its famous shop in Regent Street in 1881 with five

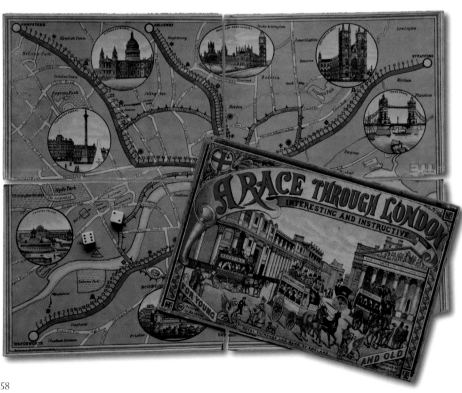

floors dedicated to toys. There were wooden toys such as large rocking-horses and Noah's Arks or toy zoos complete with animals; there were metal toys such as lead soldiers, railway engines and boats with clockwork mechanisms to make them move. There were model theatres, model shops and model forts. And there were wooden dolls, dolls with porcelain faces and real hair, dolls that cried 'Mama', peg dolls for poorer girls and dolls' houses and dolls' clothes. One toy-seller remarked, 'as long as there are children … there will always be purchasers of dolls.'

Board-games and cards became very popular at this time. Old favourites included draughts, chess and backgammon, but the new board-games were typically Victorian in that they often had a moral aim, or were educational. Snakes and Ladders, for instance, was adapted from an ancient Indian game used to teach moral behaviour, with the ladders on the virtues and the snakes on the vices. Board-games used a teetotum – a spinning-top with numbers – instead of dice, since dice were associated with gambling. Likewise, children were not given an ordinary deck of cards to play with as it might encourage gambling, but were allowed to play with special decks of cards. To begin with most children's card-games were educational and helped them learn about maths, history and science – or even cooking! But later fun card-games, with colourful decks, were invented, such as Old Maid, Happy Families and Snap.

Just as toys and games were produced specifically for children, so were books and magazines. At first moral tales were the child's fare but as demand grew, writers turned their hand to more imaginative children's works and several classics were born, including Edward Lear's *Book of Nonsense* (1846), *The Water Babies* (1864), *Alice's Adventures in Wonderland* (1865), *Black Beauty* (1877) and *Treasure Island* (1883). The newly perfected woodblock printing process enabled children's books to be attractively illustrated and several excellent artists rose to the challenge. With the publication in 1879 of *Under the Window*, a collection of drawings and verses, Kate Greenaway became one of the first artists to give children well-drawn colour illustrations in well-designed books; Beatrix Potter was to follow suit at the turn of the century.

Boys were given lead soldiers and war-games to play with, to foster interest in suitably male topics. This game, 'Storming the Castle', dates from the 1890s and may reflect the Boer War.

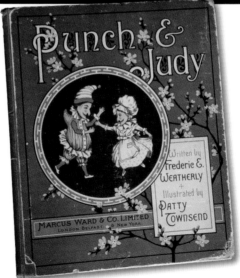

Above: This card-game introduced children to different occupations. A huckster was a person who sold wares or provisions in the street.

Left: Improved technology of printing, especially in colour, made books cheaper to produce and illustrated books like *Punch and Judy* (1886) sold in their thousands.

The Children's Friend, (far right) published from 1824 to 1930, was a monthly magazine with religious overtones, encouraging Bible reading and good works.

The Girl's Own Paper (right) was a weekly magazine, first published in 1880; in its early years it achieved a mass circulation of 200,000.

Children's magazines were first published by the Sunday School Union, but in 1866, *Boys of England* was introduced as a new type of publication: an eight-page magazine that featured serial stories of derring-do costing a penny and avidly read by boys of all classes. This and its competitors were known as 'penny dreadfuls' and were deplored by middle-class parents. So in 1879 the Religious Tract Society launched the healthier *Boy's Own Paper* featuring wholesome adventure stories as well as notes on, for example, how to practise nature study; sports and games; puzzles; and essay competitions. This proved to be very popular and continued until 1967. The *Girl's Own Paper* followed in 1880, aimed at teenage girls with its emphasis on fashion, needlework and cookery as well as stories and poetry. By the end of the century, the nature of children's publishing had changed immeasurably. now appealing to all tastes and all classes.

Ice-skating was an approved winter-time leisure activity for ladies. The first artificial ice-rink, the Glaciarium, was opened in Chelsea, London, in 1876.

Reading books and magazines were indoor activities but there were plenty of outdoor amusements, even for poor children, who could enjoy free shows performed by street entertainers. Amongst the astonishing variety of these were Punch and Judy shows; street musicians such as hurdy-gurdy players or the organ-grinder and his monkey collecting pennies; performing animals such as flea-circuses and dancing dogs; pavement artists and

This is a hand-painted slide for use in a magic lantern. In the late nineteenth century electricity replaced oil lamps and paraffin burners as the light source for the lantern.

silhouette cutters; jugglers, acrobats and sword-swallowers; curiosities like the bearded woman, and a host of other strange and wonderful things. Besides this there were the touring fairs and circuses; children could watch as the circus came to town with its caged lions, elephants, and other exotics, and the poorer children could earn free tickets by handing out notices. There were also parades on special occasions like the Queen's Jubilee in 1887 celebrating Victoria's fifty years on the throne. A visit to the theatre was also popular and the Christmas pantomime was a favourite. In the provinces plays were performed by travelling companies, but big towns and cities had their own permanent playhouses. In the 1890s, the magic-lantern show reached its peak of popularity. It could be shown at home or in a hall accompanied by narration and music, and remained the favourite form of entertainment until the early part of the twentieth century, when film took over.

Well-to-do families had the space to entertain themselves at home, with a magic-lantern show, and playing board-games and parlour games like charades and twenty questions. Every girl was required to learn the piano for the entertainment of family and visitors, when she might accompany someone who could sing or people who wanted to dance. And children had time to indulge in hobbies such as stamp-collecting and making scrapbooks.

Playing the piano was an important social skill for girls, who were able to entertain people at family gatherings.

During the nineteenth century attitudes to children changed, and by the end of it, there were laws in place to protect children from exploitation, to educate them up to a certain point and to recognise their need for a childhood. The latter meant that children had some time at least partly free from responsibilities to workplace or family, when they could play, have fun and do the things that appealed to them. While the market for leisure pastimes grew, the cost of manufacture lessened and so there were many toys, board-games and books produced just for children, to which even the poor had access.

Children made scrapbooks from pictures cut from cards and magazines or bought commercially produced scraps with images of, for example, children or flowers.

The game of lawn tennis became an outdoor sport in 1873 and was taken up socially by families.

INDEX